Gatsby COCKTAILS

Gatsby
COCKTAILS

CLASSIC COCKTAILS
FROM THE JAZZ AGE

RYLAND PETERS & SMALL
LONDON • NEW YORK

Designers Luis Peral-Aranda, Toni Kay
Editors Ellen Parnavelas, Miriam Catley
Head of Production Patricia Harrington
Art Director Leslie Harrington
Editorial Director Julia Charles
Indexer Hilary Bird
Publisher Cindy Richards

First published in 2012
This edition published in 2019
by Ryland Peters & Small
20–21 Jockey's Fields
London WC1R 4BW
and
341 E 116th St
New York NY 10029
www.rylandpeters.com

The recipes in this book have
been published previously by
Ryland Peters & Small.

10 9 8 7 6 5 4

Recipe text © Ben Reed 2012, 2019.
All other text © Ryland Peters & Small
2012, 2019.
Design, photographs and commissioned
illustrations © Ryland Peters & Small
2012, 2019. For other picture credits
please see page 64.

The author's moral rights have been
asserted. All rights reserved. No part
of this publication may be reproduced,
stored in a retrieval system or transmitted
in any form or by any means, electronic,
mechanical, photocopying or otherwise,
without the prior permission of the publisher.

ISBN: 978 1 78879 123 6

A CIP record for this book is available
from the British Library.
Library of Congress Cataloging-in-
Publication data has been applied for.

Printed in China

NOTES
• When using slices of citrus fruit such
as lemons or oranges in a drink, try to
find organic, unwaxed fruits and wash
well before using. If you can only find
treated fruit, scrub well in warm soapy
water and rinse before using.
• Measurements are occasionally given
in barspoons, which are equivalent to
5 ml or 1 teaspoon.

MIX
Paper | Supporting
responsible forestry
FSC® C008047

CONTENTS

THE GOLDEN AGE OF COCKTAILS

It was during the Prohibition era, which ran from 1920–1933, that cocktails really came into their own. Although the golden age of cocktails was probably between 1860 and 1920, it was arguably in the roaring 1920s that cocktails became very popular.

The Great Gatsby is F. Scott Fitzgerald's iconic novel, set in the 1920s at the height of the Prohibition era. It was a time of glamorous parties where bootleggers made millions selling their highly coveted illegally produced alcohol. *The Great Gatsby* is centred around one such bootlegger by the name of Jay Gatsby. In the novel, Gatsby is the mysterious host of many extravagant parties from the parlours of his luxurious mansion on Long Island, New York. There, he plays host to guests who have travelled far and wide to enjoy sipping cocktails and dancing under the stars until the sun comes up.

It seems rather unfortunate that this happy time in the development of the cocktail coincided with a most unhappy state of affairs in the USA. The Prohibition had a number of effects on drinking culture. It forced drinkers underground into illicit bars known as speakeasies, or decadent private parties such as those hosted by Jay Gatsby. These locations weren't dives, though – quite the opposite; they were luxurious and lavishly decorated and very female-friendly, which lent additional glamour to cocktails. Because liquor was illegal, inferior bootleg, or moonshine, was drunk, but was often so vile that bartenders would mix it with juices and cordials to mask its flavour. This was one of the reasons that cocktails became so popular. Many of the cocktails from this era were given seemingly innocuous names designed to fool the authorities, such as the Silk Stocking. Drinks would often be served in tea cups in an effort to disguise them from the police force.

Those bartenders who didn't wish to break the law during Prohibition hotfooted it to Cuba, or even further afield to Europe to ply their trade anew in a different country, but with as much enthusiasm as ever. This was a particularly creative time for them. Many of the drinks we count as classics today, from the Bloody Mary to the Sidecar, were invented overseas during that period, with the names of the bartenders who created them still hallowed in bars around the globe.

President Franklin D. Roosevelt had other ideas about Prohibition and it was repealed in 1933, shortly after he came to office. An accomplished drinker and handy bartender himself, FDR, along with Winston Churchill, was a great advocator of, among other cocktails, the martini. Indeed, it was during a summit meeting between Joseph Stalin, Churchill and Roosevelt in 1943 that Roosevelt first whipped up a round of Dirty Martinis for his companions.

Throughout the 20th century the cocktail has been through booms and slumps in popularity. It has adapted to social phenomena such as Prohibition, war, rises and falls of the stock market and the power of the media, and still flourishes in the 21st century, constantly evolving to suit our thirst for something new and different.

The glamour of the cocktail comes to life in this collection of authentic recipes from the 20s and 30s. Perfect the art of mixing period cocktails inspired by *The Great Gatsby*. Try serving up Jay Gatsby's tipple of choice the cooling Mint Julep, the classic Sazerac, or famous 1920s New York beverage, the Manhattan. Whether entertaining a few friends at home or hosting an extravagant Prohibition-style party of your very own, dust off your cocktail shaker and re-live the speakeasy experience with this collection of deliciously authentic cocktails.

JAZZ AGE CLASSICS

'IN HIS BLUE GARDENS MEN AND
GIRLS CAME AND WENT LIKE MOTHS
AMONG THE WHISPERINGS AND THE
CHAMPAGNE AND THE STARS.'

The Great Gatsby

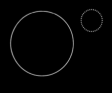
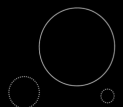

SAZERAC

ONE OF THE EARLIEST RECORDED COCKTAILS,
THE SAZERAC CAME INTO THIS WORLD SOME TIME IN
THE 1850S. IT WAS ORIGINALLY MADE WITH BRANDY,
BUT (AS I'M SURE YOU'LL AGREE) THERE'S NOTHING
QUITE LIKE A GOOD RYE WHISKEY.

• • •

50 ml/2 oz. rye whiskey

10 ml/2 barspoons sugar syrup

2 dashes Peychaud's bitters

10 ml/2 barspoons absinthe,
to rinse the glass

a thin lemon zest, to garnish

Serves 1

• • •

Stir all the ingredients, except the absinthe, in a mixing glass
filled with ice. Rinse a chilled rocks glass with the absinthe.
Strain the contents of the mixing glass into the rocks
glass and garnish with a thin zest of lemon.

SIDECAR

THE SIDECAR, LIKE MANY OF THE CLASSIC COCKTAILS
CREATED IN THE 1920S, IS ATTRIBUTED TO THE INVENTIVE
GENIUS OF HARRY MCELHONE, WHO FOUNDED
HARRY'S NEW YORK BAR LOCATED IN PARIS. IT IS SAID
TO HAVE BEEN CREATED IN HONOUR OF AN
ECCENTRIC MILITARY MAN WHO WOULD ROLL
UP OUTSIDE THE BAR IN THE SIDECAR OF HIS
CHAUFFEUR-DRIVEN MOTORCYCLE.

• • •

50 ml/2 oz. brandy

20 ml/1 oz. fresh lemon juice

20 ml/1 oz. Cointreau

sugar, for the glass

Serves 1

• • •

Shake all the ingredients together over ice and strain
into a chilled martini glass with a sugared edge.

PERFECT MANHATTAN

THIS DELICIOUS COCKTAIL HAILS FROM THE BIG CITY
JUST ACROSS THE WATER FROM JAY GATSBY'S LONG
ISLAND HOME. 'PERFECT' DESCRIBES THE PERFECT
BALANCE BETWEEN SWEET AND DRY.

• • •

50 ml/2 oz. rye whiskey

12.5 ml/2 barspoons sweet vermouth

12.5 ml/2 barspoons dry vermouth

2 dashes Angostura bitters

an orange zest, to garnish

Serves 1

• • •

Add the ingredients to a mixing glass filled with ice
(first ensure all the ingredients are very cold) and stir
the mixture until chilled. Strain into a chilled cocktail
glass, add the garnish and serve.

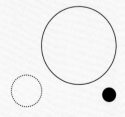

OLD FASHIONED

DURING THE PROHIBITION ERA, STRONG FLAVOURINGS SUCH AS ANGOSTURA BITTERS WERE USED IN COCKTAILS TO DISGUISE THE TASTE OF ILLEGALLY-PRODUCED SPIRITS, OTHERWISE KNOWN AS 'MOONSHINE'.

• • •

1 sugar cube

2 dashes Angostura bitters

50 ml/2 oz. rye whiskey or bourbon

an orange zest, to garnish

Serves 1

• • •

Muddle all the ingredients in a rocks glass, adding ice as you go. Garnish with an orange zest and serve.

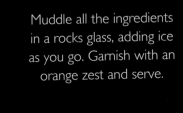

GIN GIMLET

A GREAT PARTY COCKTAIL TO SERVE ON A WARM
SUMMER'S EVENING WHILE ENTERTAINING OUTDOORS –
THIS DRINK NEEDS TO BE SHAKEN HARD TO ENSURE
A SHARP FREEZING ZESTINESS.

• • •

50 ml/2 oz. gin

25 ml/1 oz. lime cordial

Serves 1

• • •

Add the gin and cordial to a shaker filled with ice.
Shake very sharply and strain into a frosted martini glass

SILVER BRONX

THE BRONX DATES BACK TO THE DAYS OF PROHIBITION, WHEN GANG BOSSES REIGNED AND BOOZE PLAYED AN IMPORTANT PART IN THE ECONOMY OF THE UNDERWORLD. DIFFERENT AREAS OF NEW YORK BECAME KNOWN FOR THE SPECIAL COCKTAILS THEY OFFERED, SUCH AS THIS SPECIALITY OF THE BRONX.

• • •

50 ml/2 oz. gin

a dash of dry vermouth

a dash of sweet vermouth

50 ml/2 oz. fresh orange juice

1 egg white

Serves 1

• • •

Shake all the ingredients vigorously over ice and strain into a chilled cocktail glass.

SILK STOCKING

THIS TEQUILA DRINK WAS INVENTED DURING THE
1920S, AT A TIME WHEN COCKTAILS WERE OFTEN
GIVEN DECORATIVE NAMES REVELLING IN
INNUENDO AND SENSUALITY.

• • •

35 ml/¾ oz. tequila

15 ml/½ oz. white crème de cacao

1 barspoon grenadine

15 ml/½ oz. double/heavy cream

2 fresh raspberries, to garnish

Serves 1

• • •

Add all the ingredients to a blender. Add two scoops
of crushed ice and blend for 20 seconds. Pour the mixture
into a hurricane glass, garnish with two raspberries
and serve with two straws.

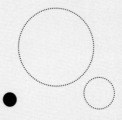

JULEPS & SMASHES

'I BELIEVE THAT ON THE FIRST NIGHT
I WENT TO GATSBY'S HOUSE I WAS
ONE OF THE FEW GUESTS WHO HAD
ACTUALLY BEEN INVITED. PEOPLE WERE
NOT INVITED—THEY WENT THERE.'

The Great Gatsby

MINT JULEP

THIS GRANDDADDY OF COCKTAILS WAS A FAVOURITE AMONG THE GUESTS AT JAY GATSBY'S INFAMOUS PARTIES. THESE DAYS IT'S A COCKTAIL FOR THE MORE DISCERNING AMONGST US.

• • •

5 ml/½ oz. sugar syrup

3 mint sprigs

60 ml/2 oz. bourbon

Serves 1

• • •

Muddle the sugar, one mint sprig and the bourbon in a rocks glass. Add crushed ice and garnish with the remaining mint sprigs. Serve with two straws.

CHAMPAGNE JULEP

ADD A TOUCH OF SPARKLE TO YOUR EVENING WITH THIS DELIGHTFUL ALTERNATIVE TO THE TRADITIONAL MINT JULEP. IF YOU HAVE A BOTTLE OF BUBBLY THAT HAS BEEN OPEN FOR A WHILE AND LOST A BIT OF ITS FIZZ, DON'T WORRY; THE SUGAR IN THE RECIPE WILL REVITALIZE IT.

• • •

5–10 sprigs of mint, plus 1 to garnish

15 ml/1 tablespoon sugar syrup

1 dash lime juice

champagne, to top up

Serves 1

• • •

Muddle the mint, sugar syrup and lime juice together in a highball glass. Add crushed ice and the champagne (gently) and stir well. Garnish with a mint sprig and serve.

MOJITO

THE MOJITO ORIGINATED IN CUBA AND IS THE
PERFECT DRINK FOR COOLING OFF AFTER A NIGHT
PERFECTING THE FAST AND FURIOUS CHARLESTON
ON THE DANCEFLOOR.

• • •

5 mint sprigs

50 ml/2 oz. golden rum

20 ml/1 oz. fresh lime juice

10 ml/scant 1 tablespoon sugar syrup

soda water, to top up

Serves 1

• • •

Put the mint in a highball glass, add the rum,
lime juice and sugar syrup and pound with a barspoon
until the aroma of the mint is released. Add crushed
ice and stir vigorously until the mixture and the
mint is spread evenly. Top with soda water
and stir again. Serve with straws.

BOURBON COBBLER

FOR A DELICIOUSLY TROPICAL ALTERNATIVE
TO A MINT JULEP, TRY A REFRESHING BOURBON
COBBLER. GENTLY EASE THE JUICE OUT OF
THE FRUIT FOR A SHARP CITRUS FLAVOUR.

• • •

a pineapple slice

an orange slice

a lemon slice

50 ml/2 oz. bourbon

15 ml/½ oz. orange curaçao

a mint sprig, to garnish

Serves 1

• • •

Gently muddle the fruit in a rocks glass, add the
bourbon, curaçao and ice and stir well. Add more ice
and stir again, garnish with a sprig of mint and
serve with two short straws.

CHAMPAGNE COBBLER

TO CREATE A PERFECT PARTY COCKTAIL, ADD
A TOUCH OF SPARKLE TO YOUR COBBLER BY
REPLACING THE BOURBON WITH CHAMPAGNE.
IF THE FRUIT IS NOT AS RIPE AS IT COULD BE,
ADD A DASH MORE SUGAR SYRUP TO
ENCOURAGE THE FLAVOUR.

• • •

a pineapple slice

an orange wheel

a lemon wheel

1 dash sugar syrup

champagne, to top up

a mint sprig, to garnish

Serves 1

• • •

Muddle the fruit together in a rocks glass. Add crushed
ice and the sugar syrup and gently top with champagne.
Stir gently and garnish with a mint sprig.

MARTINIS & APERITIFS

AND I LIKE LARGE PARTIES. THEY'RE SO INTIMATE. AT SMALL PARTIES THERE ISN'T ANY PRIVACY.'

The Great Gatsby

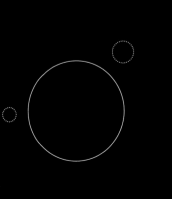
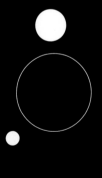

ORIGINAL DAIQUIRI

THIS CLASSIC COCKTAIL WAS MADE FAMOUS AT THE EL FLORIDITA RESTAURANT, HAVANA, EARLY IN THE 20TH CENTURY. ONCE YOU HAVE FOUND THE PERFECT BALANCE OF GOLDEN RUM (TRADITIONALLY CUBAN), SHARP CITRUS JUICE AND SWEET SUGAR SYRUP, STICK TO THOSE MEASUREMENTS EXACTLY.

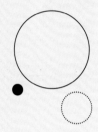

• • •

50 ml/2 oz. light rum

20 ml/1 oz. fresh lime juice

2 barspoons sugar syrup

Serves 1

• • •

Pour all the ingredients into an ice-filled shaker. Shake and strain into a chilled martini glass.

HEMINGWAY DAIQUIRI

LEGEND HAS IT THAT ERNEST HEMINGWAY WAS DIABETIC, SO THIS PARTICULAR DRINK WAS DEVISED FOR HIM USING MARASCHINO LIQUEUR AS A SWEETENER (THE SUGAR WAS RETURNED TO THE DRINK WHEN MADE FOR ANYONE OTHER THAN THE MAN HIMSELF!).

• • •

35 ml/¾ oz. white rum

15 ml/½ oz. maraschino liqueur

10 ml/2 barspoons
grapefruit juice

10 ml/2 barspoons fresh
lime juice

Serves 1

• • •

Add all the ingredients to a shaker filled with ice, shake sharply and strain into a chilled martini glass.

ORANGE DAIQUIRI

THE ORANGE DAIQUIRI SUBSTITUTES THE
SWEET MARTINIQUE RUM CALLED CREOLE SHRUB
FOR THE CUBAN RUM OF THE ORIGINAL DAIQUIRI
SO USES A LITTLE LESS SUGAR SYRUP TO KEEP
THAT DELICATE BALANCE OF SHARP AND SWEET.

• • •

50 ml/2 oz. Creole Shrub rum

20 ml/1 oz. fresh lime juice

1 barspoon sugar syrup

Serves 1

• • •

Pour all the ingredients into
an ice-filled shaker. Shake
and strain into a chilled
coupette glass.

CLASSIC MARTINI

THE CLASSIC MARTINI IS THE MOST ICONIC OF
ALL APERITIFS. STIRRING THE COCKTAIL TO MAKE
THE PERFECT MIX IS THE ORIGINAL LABOUR
OF LOVE FOR ANY BARTENDER.

• • •

a dash of vermouth
(Noilly Prat or Martini Extra Dry)

75 ml/2 ½ oz.

well-chilled gin or vodka

an olive or lemon twist,
to garnish

Serves 1

• • •

Add both the ingredients to a mixing glass
filled with ice and stir. Strain into a chilled
martini glass and garnish with an olive
or lemon twist.

DIRTY MARTINI

THIS MARTINI IS ALSO KNOWN AS THE FDR AFTER THE MAN WHO CALLED AN END TO PROHIBITION IN THE 1930S. FITTINGLY, THE GREAT PRESIDENT WAS AN ACCOMPLISHED BARTENDER WHO LOVED NOTHING MORE THAN FLOURISHING HIS SHAKER FOR ANY HEAD OF STATE WITH A LIKE MIND OR A DRY PALATE.

• • •

50 ml/2 oz. gin

1 dash dry vermouth

12.5 ml/2 barspoons olive brine

a lemon zest, for the glass

a green olive, to garnish

Serves 1

• • •

Add the gin, dry vermouth and olive brine to a shaker filled with cracked ice. Shake sharply and strain into a chilled martini glass with a lemon-zested edge. Garnish with an olive.

SMOKY MARTINI

THE MARTINI HAS SO MANY DELICIOUS VARIATIONS.
TRY USING A VERY SMOKY MALT, SUCH AS TALISKER,
OR A PEATED ONE, SUCH AS LAPHROAIG,
FOR INTERESTING RESULTS.

• • •

50 ml/2 oz. gin

1 dash dry vermouth

1 dash whiskey

a lemon zest, to garnish

Serves 1

• • •

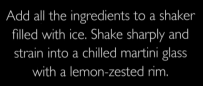

Add all the ingredients to a shaker
filled with ice. Shake sharply and
strain into a chilled martini glass
with a lemon-zested rim.

GIBSON

THE LEADING THEORY BEHIND THE ORIGIN OF
THIS CLASSIC MARTINI IS THAT IT WAS FIRST MADE
AT THE BEGINNING OF THE 20TH CENTURY FOR
CHARLES GIBSON, A FAMOUS ILLUSTRATOR,
AT THE PLAYER'S CLUB IN NEW YORK.

• • •

1 dash vermouth
(Noilly Prat or
Martini Extra Dry)

75 ml/2½ oz. well-chilled
gin or vodka

silverskin onions,
to garnish

Serves 1

• • •

Add both the ingredients to a mixing glass filled with ice
and stir. Strain into a chilled martini glass and garnish with
a few silverskin onions skewered on a cocktail stick.

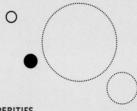

RICKEYS & FIZZES

'I WAS ENJOYING MYSELF NOW.
I HAD TAKEN TWO FINGER BOWLS
OF CHAMPAGNE AND THE SCENE
HAD CHANGED BEFORE MY EYES
INTO SOMETHING SIGNIFICANT,
ELEMENTAL AND PROFOUND.'

The Great Gatsby

RASPBERRY RICKEY

THE RICKEY ORIGINATED IN WASHINGTON D.C.
IN THE 1880S. IT WAS TRADITIONALLY MADE WITH GIN
OR BOURBON WHISKEY, SODA WATER AND A LITTLE
LIME JUICE. HERE, SOME RASPBERRY LIQUEUR AND
FRESH RASPBERRIES HAVE BEEN ADDED TO ADD A SPLASH
OF COLOUR AND A BEAUTIFUL BERRY FLAVOUR.

• • •

4 fresh raspberries

50 ml/2 oz. vodka

20 ml/1 oz. fresh
lime juice

1 dash Chambord

soda water, to top up

a lime wedge, to garnish

Serves 1

• • •

Muddle the raspberries in the bottom of a highball
glass. Fill with ice, add the remaining ingredients
and stir gently. Garnish with a lime wedge
and serve with two straws.

SLOE GIN FIZZ

THE GIN FIZZ BECAME VERY POPULAR IN THE UNITED
STATES BETWEEN 1900 AND 1940. A SPECIALTY OF
NEW ORLEANS, WHERE DEMAND FOR THE DRINK
BECAME SO HIGH THAT BARTENDERS COULD
BE FOUND SHAKING THE FIZZES UNTIL THE
EARLY HOURS OF THE MORNING.

• • •

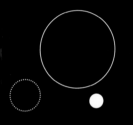

50 ml/2 oz. sloe gin

20 ml/1 oz. fresh

lemon juice

1 dash sugar syrup

soda water, to top up

a lemon slice, to garnish

Serves 1

• • •

Add all the ingredients, except the soda, to a shaker
filled with ice. Shake sharply and strain into a highball glass
filled with ice. Top with soda water, garnish with
a lemon slice and serve with two straws.

PEACH RICKEY

THIS FRESH PEACH RICKEY IS A GUARANTEED CROWD PLEASER. IT APPEALS DUE TO THE NATURE OF THE INGREDIENTS – THERE JUST SEEMS TO BE SOMETHING ABOUT PEACH PURÉE IN COCKTAILS THAT EVERYONE ENJOYS.

• • •

50 ml/2 oz. vodka

20 ml/1 oz. fresh lime juice

15 ml/½ oz. peach purée

1 dash crème de pêche

soda water, to top up

thin peach slices, to serve

Serves 1

• • •

Build all the ingredients into a highball glass filled with ice. Stir gently and garnish with a thin peach slice or two.

ROYAL GIN FIZZ

ADD A LITTLE CHAMPAGNE TO YOUR FIZZ AND YOU'VE
GOT A ROYAL GIN FIZZ — THE PERFECTLY ELEGANT
COCKTAIL TO HELP MAKE THAT OCCASION
EXTRA SPECIAL.

• • •

50 ml/2 oz. gin

25 ml/1 oz. fresh lemon juice

1 barspoon white sugar
(or 12.5 ml/½ oz. sugar syrup)

1 egg white

champagne

Serves 1

• • •

Add all the ingredients, except the champagne, to a shaker
filled with ice. Shake sharply and strain into a highball glass
filled with ice. Top with champagne and serve.

ELDERFLOWER COLLINS

THIS REFRESHING SUMMER DRINK IS A CLOSE RELATION
OF THE TOM COLLINS THAT ORIGINATED IN NEW YORK
IN THE 1880S. THE BOTANICALS IN THE GIN GET AN
UNEXPECTED BOOST FROM THE ELDERFLOWER,
MAKING THIS A DELICATE COCKTAIL FULL
OF FLORAL FLAVOURS.

• • •

50 ml/2 oz. gin

20 ml/1 oz.
fresh lemon juice

15 ml/½ oz.
elderflower cordial

soda water, to top up

sugar syrup, to taste

a lemon slice, to garnish

a mint sprig, to garnish

Serves 1

• • •

Build all the ingredients into a highball glass filled with ice.
Stir gently and garnish with a lemon slice and a sprig of mint.

INDEX

CREDITS

All photography by
William Lingwood
All illustrations by
Rob Merrett apart from:
Pages 2, 36 and 52
Images courtesy of
The Advertising Archives
Page 8 Image courtesy
of Mary Evans Picture
Library
Page 24 At the Cocktail
Party, fashion plate
from 'Art Gout Beaute'
magazine, March 1927
(pochoir print) by French
School, (20th century)
Bibliotheque des Arts
Decoratifs, Paris, France/
Archives Charmet/ The
Bridgeman Art Library/
copyright unknown.
All best efforts have been
made to trace the owner
of this image. Should you
have further information,
please contact us.